My First Pet

Cats

by Cari Meister

Bullfrog Books

Ideas for Parents and Teachers

Bullfrog Books let children practice reading informational text at the earliest reading levels. Repetition, familiar words, and photo labels support early readers.

Before Reading

- Ask the child to think about pet cats. Ask: What do you know about cats?
- Look at the picture glossary together. Read and discuss the words.

Read the Book

- "Walk" through the book and look at the photos. Let the child ask questions. Point out the photo labels.
- Read the book to the child, or have him or her read independently.

After Reading

- Prompt the child to think more. Ask: What do you need to take care of a cat or kitten? Would you like to own a cat?

Bullfrog Books are published by Jump!
5357 Penn Avenue South
Minneapolis, MN 55419
www.jumplibrary.com

Library of Congress Cataloging-in-Publication Data

Meister, Cari, author.
 Cats / by Cari Meister.
   pages cm. — (My first pet)
 Audience: 005-008.
 Audience: K to grade 3.
 Summary: "This photo-illustrated book for early readers tells how to take care of a pet cat" — Provided by publisher.
 Includes bibliographical references and index.
 ISBN 978-1-62031-121-9 (hardcover) —
 ISBN 978-1-62496-188-5 (ebook) —
 ISBN 978-1-62031-142-4 (paperback)
 1. Cats — Juvenile literature. I. Title.
 SF445.7.M45 2015
 636.8'0887—dc23
                                    2013042368

Series Editor: Rebecca Glaser
Series Designer: Ellen Huber
Book Designer: Anna Peterson
Photo Researcher: Casie Cook

Photo Credits: All photos by Shutterstock except: Arthur Tilley/Getty, 8–9; Steve Lyne/Getty, 12; Juniors/SuperStock, 12–13; Monkey Business Images/Dreamstime.com, 15; Corbis/SuperStock, 16–17; Hulya Ozkok/Getty, 18–19; jml5571/iStock, 22

Printed in the United States of America at Corporate Graphics, in North Mankato, Minnesota.
3-2014
10 9 8 7 6 5 4 3 2 1

Table of Contents

A Lot of Cats!

Ana wants a cat.

She goes to a shelter.

Look at all the cats!

5

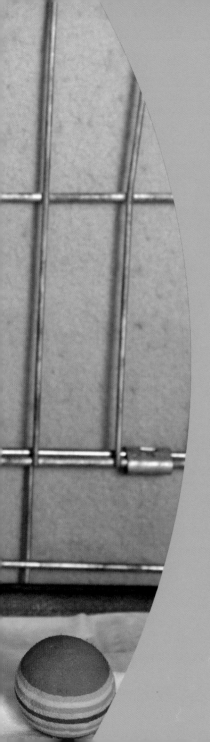

Ana asks about each cat.

Then she sees Max.

"Meow!"

She brings him home.

Lots of people have a cat.

Tyler holds his kitten.

He pets her.

She purrs.

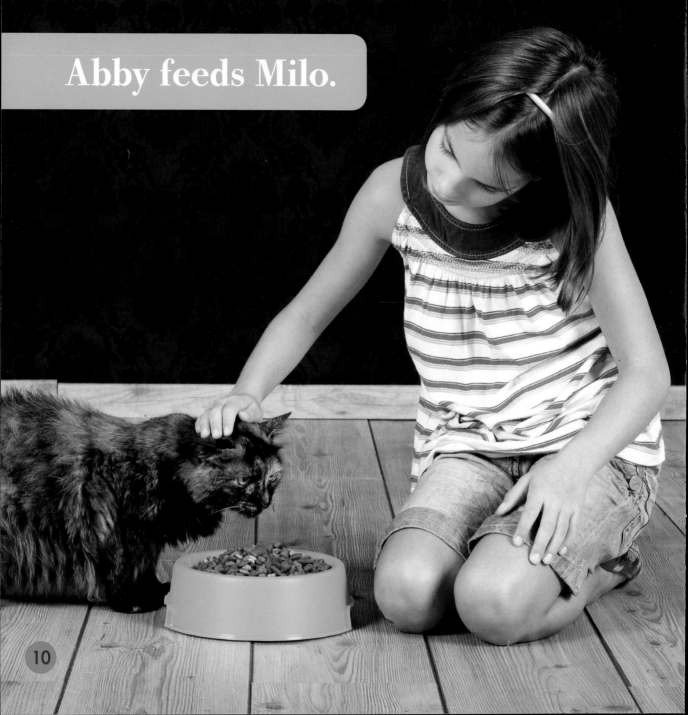

Abby feeds Milo.

She gives him food.
She fills his water dish.

Emma cleans the litter box.

She scoops the poop every day.

litter box

Lucas gives Zoe a collar and tag.
The tag has his phone number.

collar

tag

If Zoe gets lost,
people will call him.

vet

Gus takes Sky to the vet.

The vet checks Sky.

He gives her shots.

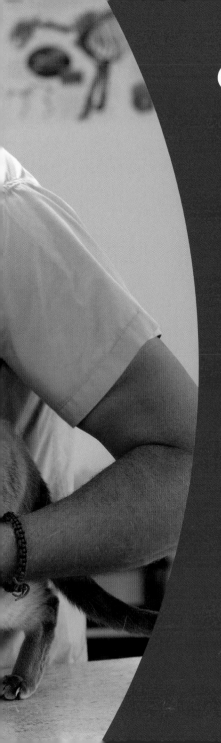

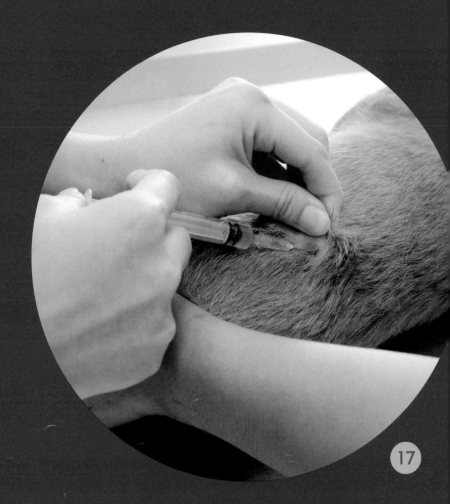

Ted gives Beast
a catnip mouse.

It makes Beast go crazy!

catnip
toy

Cats make fun pets!

What Does a Cat Need?

collar
A band that goes around a cat's neck and holds a tag.

scratching post
Cats like to scratch their claws on these posts.

cat food
Cat food has all the nutrition your pet needs.

water dish
Cats need fresh, clean water every day.

Picture Glossary

catnip
A plant that some cats react to that is used in cat toys.

shelter
A place where people take care of animals that do not have homes.

litter box
A box used by a cat to go potty.

vet
An animal doctor.

Index

To Learn More

Learning more is as easy as 1, 2, 3.

1) Go to www.factsurfer.com

2) Enter "pet cat" into the search box.

3) Click the "Surf" button to see a list of websites.

With factsurfer.com, finding more information is just a click away.